Dreams

Dreams

The Story of Martin Luther King, Jr.

by

Peter Murray

Illustrated by

Robin Lawrie

The Child's World®

Library of Congress Cataloging-in-Publication Data
Murray, Peter, 1952 Sept. 29–
Dreams: the story of Martin Luther King, Jr. / Peter Murray.
p. cm.
Summary: A biography of the Baptist minister who spent
much of his life pursuing his dream of equal treatment
for fellow African Americans and for all people.
ISBN 1-56766-223-4 (hardcover : library bound)
1. King, Martin Luther, Jr., 1929-1968—Juvenile literature.
2. Afro-Americans—Biography—Juvenile literature.
3. Baptists—United States—Clergy—Biography—Juvenile literature.
4. Civil rights workers—United States—Biography—Juvenile literature.
5. Dreams—Juvenile literature.
[1. King, Martin Luther, Jr., 1929-1968. 2. Civil rights workers.
3. Clergy. 4. Civil rights movements—History. 5. Afro-Americans—Biography.]
I. Title.
E185.97.K5M87   1998
323'.092—dc20
[B]
95-43789
CIP
AC

Contents

 M.L. 6

College Years 12

Montgomery 14

Rosa Parks 16

Sit-ins and Freedom Rides 20

Birmingham 22

I Have a Dream 24

Study Guide 28

Study Guide Answers 30

One August day in 1935, five-year-old M.L. went across the street to see two of his friends. He had been playing with them all summer. M.L. was excited. In a few days, he would be going to school for the very first time!

A little while later, M.L. came running home in tears.

"What's wrong?" his mother asked. "Are you hurt?"

M.L. shook his head.

"What happened?" his mother asked.

"They won't play with me no more," M.L. sobbed.

Mrs. King sighed. She had known this would happen sooner or later.

M.L.'s full name was Martin Luther King, Junior, but everybody called him M.L. He was a handsome boy. He had curly dark hair, skin the color of fine chocolate, and quick, intelligent eyes.

His two friends were white boys. Their mother said it wasn't right for them to be playing with a little black boy. She told them they were starting school now, and they should play with their own kind.

M.L. didn't understand. He wondered, *What's wrong with me? Why don't they like me anymore?*

Mrs. King wiped away his tears and said, "M.L., I'm going to tell you something. Are you listening?"

M.L. nodded.

His mother said, "You are just as good as anybody."

On December 13, 1865, slavery was outlawed in the United States. But the African American people who had been slaves were not truly free. Southern states had "Jim Crow Laws" designed to keep blacks and whites apart. Blacks were discouraged from voting. They weren't allowed to have good jobs. Black children went to separate, poorer schools. In later years, blacks had to ride in the back of the bus. They had to sit in the balcony at movie theaters.

They had to drink from separate water fountains. Keeping blacks and whites apart is called *segregation*.

For nearly one hundred years after the end of slavery, African Americans continued to suffer from unfair laws. In 1935, the idea of "civil rights" seemed like an impossible dream.

I have a dream that my four little children will one day live in a nation where they will not be judged by the color of their skin, but by the content of their character. I have a dream that one day. . .little black boys and black girls will be able to join hands with little white boys and white girls as sisters and brothers. *I have a dream today!*

—Martin Luther King, Jr., from his *I Have a Dream* speech

Martin Luther King, Jr., grew up in a big house in Atlanta, Georgia. His father, the Reverend Martin Luther King, Sr., was the pastor of the Ebenezer Baptist Church. The King family was respected in their neighborhood. Reverend King spoke out against segregation. He told the people in his church that it was wrong to segregate blacks because of the color of their skin. He was one of the first people to join the National Association for the Advancement of Colored People (NAACP). He spoke out against the Jim Crow Laws.

Some white people accused the Reverend King of being "uppity" and a "troublemaker." In those days, it was dangerous for African American people to speak out for their rights. Being "uppity" could get you killed!

One day Reverend King took M.L. downtown to buy a pair of shoes. They sat down in the front row of seats. The shoe salesman asked them to move to the seats in the back row. The front seats were for "whites only."

Reverend King refused to move. "Nothing wrong with these seats," he said.

"I can't help you unless you move to the back," the shoe salesman said.

Reverend King took M.L. by the hand and left the store. He wouldn't do business with anyone who did not treat him fairly. He wasn't afraid to stand up to white people. "You can't be afraid of doing what's right," he said.

M.L. would remember that for the rest of his life.

M.L. loved to hear his father speak in church.
When Reverend King spoke, people listened.
His words gave people hope and strength.
M.L. learned that words were a powerful tool.
He was only a little boy, but one day he turned
to his mother and said, "When I grow up,

I'm going to get me some big words, too."

M.L. was already dreaming of the future. He saw that with the
right words, he could do anything.

As he grew into a teenager, M.L.'s voice became strong and
deep. He loved to read, and he loved to talk. He got himself some
"big words." At the age of 15, he won a speech contest in another
city, 90 miles from home.

After the contest he rode home on the bus with his teacher,
Mrs. Bradley. It should have been a joyful ride, but the bus driver
made M.L. and his teacher give up their
seats so that some white people could
sit down. When they didn't move
quickly enough, the driver cursed
them and called them names.
They had to ride all the way back
to Atlanta standing up.

Years later, he wrote, "It was
the angriest I've ever been in
my life."

College Years

As Martin Luther King, Jr., grew older, he saw more and more discrimination against African Americans. He began to see white people as his enemies. His father preached that you should forgive your enemies, but M.L. was often too angry to forgive. He dreamed of a day when blacks would go to the best public schools, work at good jobs, and sit at the front of the bus. He was not content to sit back and wait for his dream to come true.

I see a ray of hope, but I am different from my father. I feel the need of being free *now!*
—*Martin Luther King, Jr., in a letter to Robert Kennedy*

In 1944, when he was only 15 years old, King entered Morehouse College in Atlanta. At first, he wanted to be a doctor. But a doctor can only help one person at a time. He decided to become a minister like his father. As a minister, his words could reach thousands of people. He dreamed of having his own church where he could preach the Word of God. He wanted to help black Americans live their lives with pride and dignity. He wanted to fight discrimination.

While he was in college, King learned about the Indian leader Mahatma Gandhi. Gandhi's people had been discriminated against, too. But instead of getting angry, Gandhi forgave his enemies. He battled discrimination by refusing to obey the unfair laws. When Gandhi and his followers were arrested and thrown in jail, they did not fight back. This type of protest is called *civil disobedience.*

Gandhi was sent to prison many times. Thousands of his followers were also imprisoned. But the government of India couldn't put *everybody* in jail! After years of civil disobedience, Gandhi and his people won their freedom and their civil rights.

King read everything he could find about Mahatma Gandhi. Could Gandhi's peaceful way help African Americans win their civil rights?

Montgomery

In 1953, King married Coretta Scott. When King finished college, he and Coretta had to decide where they would live. He could go on to teach college, or he could become the pastor of a church. It was not a hard decision, because Martin Luther King had a dream!

"I want to be the pastor of a church," he told his new wife. "A large Baptist church in the South."

"Why in the South?" she asked. Coretta did not want to live in the South. She did not want to live under the Jim Crow Laws. She did not want to be treated like a second-class citizen.

King told her, "I want to live in the South because that is where I'm needed."

King took a job as pastor of the Dexter Avenue Baptist Church in Montgomery, Alabama. The city was so segregated that it was against the law for blacks and whites to play checkers together!

King preached against the Jim Crow Laws. He told his people to stand up for their rights. He taught them to be proud. He told them they were as good as anybody.

But these were only words. He knew that one day he would have to challenge the Jim Crow Laws in court. He was waiting for a case that would show the nation just how wrong it was to segregate people by the color of their skin.

Rosa Parks

It was December 1, 1955. Rosa Parks had worked all day. All she wanted was to go home and rest. She climbed aboard a city bus. Because she was black, she had to sit in the back of the bus. The bus filled up with people. Some white people got on, but there were no seats left. The driver told Rosa to stand up and give her seat to a white man.

Rosa was in no mood to be pushed around. It wasn't fair. She was tired. Her feet hurt. Rosa Parks refused to move!

The bus driver stopped the bus and called the police. Rosa Parks was arrested and put in jail.

The story quickly spread through Montgomery's black community. The next day, word of Rosa Parks reached King. This was what he had been waiting for. King and other members of the NAACP organized a *boycott* to protest the Montgomery bus laws. A *boycott* is when a group of people refuse to buy something. They spread the word to every black person in the city. Do not ride the buses! If they were not treated equally, they would not ride. The bus company would not get any of their money.

IF WE DO NOT DO SOMETHING TO STOP THESE ARRESTS THEY WILL CONTINUE. THE NEXT TIME IT MAY BE YOU, OR YOUR DAUGHTER, OR YOUR MOTHER. . .DON'T RIDE THE BUSES TO WORK, TO TOWN, TO SCHOOL. . .

—*from a leaflet handed out after the arrest of Rosa Parks.*

The next day, the city buses were nearly empty. Day after day, the buses rolled by carrying only a few white passengers, or none at all. The bus company was losing money. Montgomery's blacks thought the boycott would be over quickly. How long could the company afford to operate empty buses?

But the bus company refused to change. They thought that the blacks needed their buses and would soon start riding again.

They were wrong. Blacks found other ways of getting to work and school. They walked, they rode bicycles, or they formed car pools. But they never, ever rode the bus.

Martin Luther King was arrested for organizing the boycott, and Rosa Parks was fined ten dollars. She refused to pay.

The case went to the Supreme Court.

The boycott lasted almost a year. On November 13, 1956, the Supreme Court ruled Alabama's bus laws were unconstitutional.

The boycott was over. One of Martin Luther King's dreams had come true. He had led his people to a great civil rights victory.

The Montgomery boycott made King famous. He had proved that civil disobedience could work in America. His people could win their rights without using violence. King traveled across the South preaching his message of peaceful resistance. He joined the Southern Christian Leadership Conference (SCLC). The purpose of the SCLC was to "fight for Negro dignity everywhere" using nonviolence.

In 1957, the SCLC organized a rally in front of the Lincoln Memorial in Washington, D.C. King spoke before an audience of 25,000 people. At the age of 28, he had become the leader of America's civil rights movement.

Sit-ins and Freedom Rides

In February of 1959, four black students sat down at a lunch counter in a North Carolina Woolworths store. They ordered food, but the waitress refused to serve them. The counter was for "whites only." The students were black. So the students just sat there, refusing to leave until the store closed.

The next day, they came back and sat at the same lunch counter. They said they would come back every day until they were served.

That is how the first "sit-in" began. Other black civil rights workers started other sit-ins. In 1960, Martin Luther King was arrested at a sit-in in Atlanta.

I have a dream that one day on the red hills of Georgia, sons of former slaves and sons of former slave holders will be able to sit down together at the table of brotherhood.
—Martin Luther King, Jr., from his *I Have a Dream* speech

It was a time of action for African Americans. In the early 1960s, most bus lines in the South were still segregated. The Freedom Riders were groups of blacks and whites who rode together on the buses, sitting wherever they wanted. At the bus stations they used "white only" restrooms, and sat in "white only" waiting areas. Many whites were furious. Some buses were burned, and many Freedom Riders were beaten by angry groups of whites. After many months, the U.S. government declared segregation on all buses and trains illegal. The Freedom Riders had won another civil rights victory!

Birmingham

Birmingham, Alabama, was one of the most segregated cities in the South. In 1963, King went to Birmingham to lead a civil rights march. But many adults in Birmingham were afraid to march, so the SCLC asked students to join their protest. Thousands of children, many of them only eight or nine years old, joined the march. They sang as they walked through the streets of the city.

"Bull" Connor, the police chief, was furious. More than nine hundred children were arrested. The police blasted them with fire hoses. They turned their police dogs loose on them. They beat them with clubs.

All over America, people saw the children being attacked. Blacks and whites were outraged! Even the policemen felt bad about what they had done.

Two days later, the children marched again. Bull Connor ordered his men to attack, but this time they refused to obey. The city agreed to end segregation in restaurants and stores. It was another great victory for the civil rights movement.

I Have a Dream

In the eight years since Rosa Parks had started the bus boycott, Martin Luther King and other civil rights workers had accomplished a great deal. But there was still work to be done. In August of 1963, a huge march was planned. Civil rights workers from all over America went to Washington, D.C. Hundreds of thousands of people gathered at the Lincoln Memorial. For two hours, one speaker after another addressed the crowd. People were getting hungry and thirsty, but they stayed to hear the greatest civil rights speaker of all.

Finally, Martin Luther King, Jr. stood before them. His powerful, clear voice rang out across the sea of people.

"I have a dream," he said.

The crowd fell silent. They had a dream, too.

"I have a dream that one day this nation will rise up and live out the true meaning of its creed, 'We hold these truths to be self evident, that all men are created equal.'"

King went on to deliver one of the greatest speeches of all time. His dream was his people's dream. With each victory of the civil rights movement, their dream came closer to reality.

Everyone who heard King speak on that historic day was inspired by his words. He ended his speech by describing his most treasured dream. He dreamed of that day when

". . . all God's children, black men and white men, Jews and gentiles, Protestants and Catholics, will be able to join hands and sing . . . 'Free at last. Free at last. Thank God almighty, we are free at last!'"

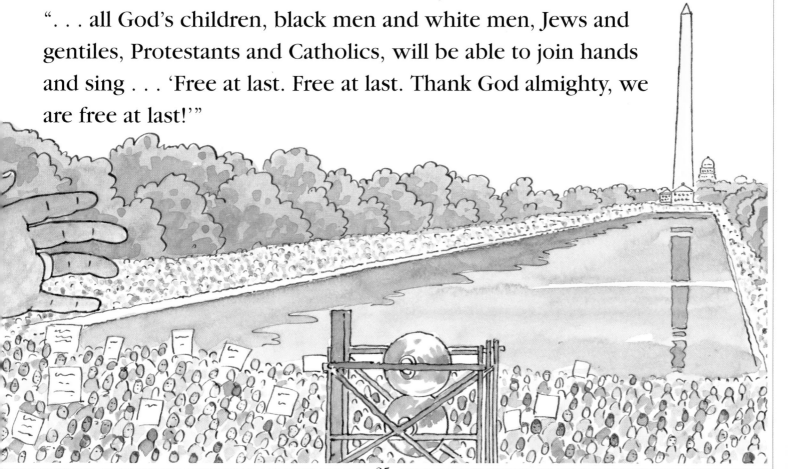

Martin Luther King's dream was greater than it had seemed. He dreamed not only of equality for African Americans. He dreamed of freedom and equality and happiness for all people, of every color and every religion.

But not everyone was happy about what King and his followers had accomplished. Many whites were angry. They wanted to keep the Jim Crow Laws. They wanted to keep blacks "in their place." King received many death threats, but he continued his civil rights work.

On April 3, 1968, he delivered a speech at a rally in Memphis, Tennessee. He spoke of life and death. He spoke of hope and dreams. At the end of his speech he said,

I've seen the Promised Land. I may not get there with you. But I want you to know tonight that we as a people will get to the Promised Land. I'm so happy tonight. I'm not worried about anything. I'm not fearing any man. "Mine eyes have seen the glory of the coming of the Lord."

Those who heard this speech were shocked! Was King speaking of his own death?

The next day, standing outside his hotel room, Martin Luther King, Jr., was shot in the head by an angry white man. He died within the hour.

Martin Luther King, Jr., has left this earth and gone to his "Promised Land." But his dream is still alive. It lives today in the hearts of all good people, both black and white. King knew that he would not live to see his dream become reality. But he had seen "the Promised Land" in his mind. He knew that the day would come when "little black boys and black girls will be able to join hands with little white boys and white girls as sisters and brothers." Martin Luther King had a dream.

Study Guide

Martin Luther King, Jr., was inspired by Mahatma Gandhi. Today, many young men and women are inspired by Martin Luther King, Jr. Reading about great men and women can teach us about how to become better people.

1. Which of these qualities do you think is most important?

Intelligence

Authentic ability

Imagination

Generosity

Humor

Patience

Courage

Strength

Fairness

Honesty

Perseverance

Curiosity

Kindness

Self-confidence

Which qualities do you think were most important to Martin Luther King, Jr.?

2. In 1957, 1964, and 1968, the U.S. government passed civil rights bills designed to protect African Americans and other minorities from discrimination. Today, blacks in America do not have to deal with Jim Crow Laws. But has discrimination ended in America?

3. Everyone dreams of the future. But not everyone works to make their dreams come true. You might dream of becoming rich and famous. You might dream of flying to outer space. You might dream of getting a new bicycle. You might dream of getting an "A" in history class. What are your dreams? What can you do to make the come true?

4. Booker T. Washington was a great black leader during the early 1900s. He once said, "Let no man pull you so low as to make you hate him." What did he mean by that? Do you think that Martin Luther King, Jr. would have agreed?

5. Many other African Americans have helped fight discrimination. Here is a list of just a few. Do you know who they are?

Jackie Robinson

Ralph Ellison

Rev. Jesse Jackson

Ralph David Abernathy

W. E. B. Du Bois

Study Guide Answers

1. Martin Luther King, Jr., knew that to be a successful person is to have many good qualities. He had to have an **education**, so that he could understand the world around him. He had to be **courageous** and **strong,** because his dreams would not come easily. He had to show **kindness**, **fairness,** and **honesty**, or people would not respect him. It was not enough for Martin Luther King, Jr., to just dream. He had to have many other qualities to make his dreams come true.

2. As long as people hold hatred and envy and anger in their hearts, discrimination will continue. Even today, African Americans and other minorities are often treated unfairly because of the color of their skin. Fortunately, because of the civil rights laws of the 1960s, people who violate someone's civil rights can now be taken to court. Discrimination is still a problem, but its victims now have the law on their side.

3. Dreams don't just happen on their own. If you sit around and wait for your dreams to come true, you'll be sitting for a long, long time. But when you work to make your dream come true, it will happen. When Martin Luther King first dreamed of having his own church, he was a little boy. It took years of hard work before he actually preached to his own congregation.

4. When we hate someone, we fill ourselves up with bad feelings. If someone calls you names or treats you unfairly, it does no good to hate them. All it does is use up your time and energy and make you feel bad. Martin Luther King, Jr., learned that if he forgave his enemies, he could concentrate on building his dreams. Hating them would accomplish nothing.

5. **Jackie Robinson** was the first black athlete to play major league baseball when he joined the Brooklyn Dodgers in 1947. Before that, black players had to play in their own league.

Ralph Ellison wrote a famous novel called <u>The Invisible Man</u>. His book told readers all over the world what it was like to be a black man in America.

Rev. Jesse Jackson worked with Martin Luther King. He was one of the last people King spoke to before he was killed. Since then, Jackson has emerged as one of the foremost civil rights activists in the United States.

Ralph David Abernathy was the pastor of Rosa Parks' church. He was one of the founders of the SCLC, and he worked closely with Martin Luther King during the 1960s.

W. E. B. Du Bois founded the Niagara Movement in 1905. Four years later, The Niagara Movement became the National Association for the Advancement of Colored People (NAACP).

Martin Luther King, Jr.

1929 January 15,   Martin Luther King, Jr., is born.

1953 King marries Coretta Scott.

1957 King is named president of the Southern Christian Leadership Conference.

1963 King leads protests in Birmingham, Alabama.

1963 August 28. King delivers his "I Have a Dream" speech in Washington, D.C.

1968 April 4. King is assassinated in Memphis, Tennessee.